To my incredible wife, Tara—

Your love, encouragement, and unwavering belief in me made this book possible. Every late night, every moment of doubt, you were there with a gentle reminder, a warm hug, and the strength I needed to keep going. Thank you for being my inspiration, and my greatest support.

Introduction

THE SENSUAL ART OF EATING

A Multi-Sensory Guide to Caloric Indulgence

Imagine this: you take a bite of food, and it's not just about the flavor dancing on your tongue. It's the way the vibrant colors of your meal pop, making your eyes linger on every plateful. It's the seductive aroma that fills the air, teasing your senses before the first taste even touches your lips. The satisfying crunch, the smooth glide of a perfectly cooked bite - each moment unfolding with every chew. Eating becomes an affair, a sensory journey that heightens every emotion, every craving. Yet, in the rush of our busy lives, we often forget that food isn't just fuel. It's an experience, a multi-sensory escape waiting to be savored.

This book is your invitation to rediscover the art of eating through all your senses. It's a celebration of the sights, smells, textures, sounds, and flavors that make every meal an adventure. By simply slowing down, we can transform eating into something sensual, nourishing, and deeply satisfying. Through mindfulness and being present, you will learn how to elevate even the simplest meals into enriching moments of pure pleasure. So, let's dive in and savor the richness of food like never before and allow every meal to be a journey worth taking.

Sight - The Visual Feast

We've all been there—standing in front of a beautifully plated dish, feeling the urge to snap a picture before even taking a bite. There's something almost magnetic about how our eyes feast before our mouths do. But why is that? Why does the way food looks seem to enhance its flavor, or even trigger our appetite? It's not just a passing fancy—there's science and psychology behind the seductive power of food presentation. In this chapter, we're diving into the visual allure of food, exploring how color, plating, and composition can elevate our eating experience, making every bite feel like a celebration of the senses.

The Power of Presentation: How the appearance of food affects appetite and taste perception.

They say we eat with our eyes first, and there's a lot of truth to that. The visual appeal of food doesn't just get us excited to dig in; it actually affects how we perceive its flavor. A well-presented dish can make us feel more indulgent, more satisfied, even before we've tasted a thing. Imagine being handed a plate of vibrant sushi—each piece delicately arranged, the fish glistening, the greens of wasabi and ginger creating a vivid contrast against the rich reds and pinks. Doesn't it just "feel" more luxurious?

It's not just in your head. Studies show that when food is presented beautifully, it activates our brain's reward centers, making us anticipate a more delicious experience. That's why plating is in itself an art form: it taps into the power of our senses and primes us for the pleasure to come.

Colors and their influence: The psychology behind the hues of food and the subtle impact they have over preference and flavor expectations.

Ever notice how the color of your food can make your mouth water—or turn your stomach? That's not just a coincidence. Color has a profound psychological effect on our food preferences and expectations. For example, red and yellow—think ripe strawberries or golden roasted potatoes—are linked to sweetness and richness. They trigger excitement and energy. Blue, on the other hand, is rare in natural foods, and it often signals a warning (like mold or spoilage). It's why we don't usually associate blue with food, unless it's artificial, like blue candy or a cocktail, which feels intriguing, almost exotic.

But here's the fun part: certain colors also shape the way we "expect" food to taste. The color of a drink, for instance, can lead us to believe it's sweeter or more sour than it actually is. That's why a perfectly pink strawberry milkshake can make us feel like we're indulging in something rich and decadent, even if it's made with skim milk. We connect those rich, inviting hues with flavor, without even tasting it yet.

Plating and Composition: Tips for enhancing the visual appeal of everyday meals.

Let's face it: presentation matters. But you don't need to be a Michelin-starred chef to make your food look irresistible. Plating is all about balance, texture, and color. Take the humble salad, for example. Instead of throwing everything into a bowl and hoping for the best, try arranging your ingredients with intention. Place bright greens in the center—like baby spinach or arugula—then add pops of color around the plate: slices of juicy tomatoes, creamy avocado, perhaps a sprinkle of pomegranate seeds. The goal is to create visual interest, guiding the eye in a way that makes the dish feel dynamic and exciting.

When it comes to texture, think of contrast. A silky smooth hummus, a crispy wedge of pita, and crunchy cucumber slices create a sensual dance for both the eyes and the palate. Don't forget the little details—an extra drizzle of olive oil, a few sprigs of fresh herbs, or a dusting of paprika can take a dish from good to sexy. It's the finishing touches that turn an everyday meal into an experience.

Smell – The Aromatic Prelude

Have you noticed that there's something undeniably seductive about the way a fragrance teases the senses. It lingers in the air, curling around you like a lover's touch, whispering promises of what's to come. Smell is the most primal of all our senses, the one that ties us intimately to memory and emotion. But more than that, it's the secret lover of taste, the unseen player in the grand symphony of flavor. Without smell, taste would be a mere shadow of itself, a dull, flat experience. When you inhale deeply before taking a bite, you're setting the stage for a sensory performance like no other, where the scent guides the flavor and elevates the pleasure.

The intimate connection between Smell and Taste: Understanding how smell affects flavor.

Think about it: the next time you take a bite of something delicious, try pausing and focusing on the way the smell wraps around you before the taste hits your tongue. Smell and taste are so closely linked, they share the same neural pathways in the brain. When we savor a dish, the scent you inhale is telling your brain exactly what to expect from the taste. It's like your taste buds and olfactory senses have a secret handshake, or a culinary "high five" smell prepares your mind to welcome the flavors, enhancing the overall experience. If you've ever had a delicious piece of fruit or a steaming bowl of soup, you'll know how the scent invites you in first, heightening anticipation before the taste even reaches your tongue. Without that aromatic prelude, the flavor would fall flat, as if you'd walked into a room and forgot to turn the lights on. It's that simple.

Our sense of smell is responsible for more than 80% of what we perceive as flavor. When we eat, the aroma from the food rises up into the nasal cavity, where it meets the olfactory receptors. These receptors send signals to the brain, which interprets the signals as taste. In other words, it's the smells that help us experience the depth and complexity of flavor. That's why eating with a cold or when your nose is blocked feels like a half-experience—because the smell is missing, and therefore so is the flavor.

Enhancing Aromas in Cooking: Simple techniques like using fresh herbs, spices, and aromatics.

Did you know that a perfume maker carefully selects notes to create a signature scent, a cook can choose ingredients that enhance the aroma of a dish. The right herbs, spices, and aromatics transform a simple meal into an unforgettable sensory experience. Fresh herbs, for instance, release oils when you chop or bruise them— think of the intoxicating fragrance of mint or basil as it's cut. Also spices like garlic, ginger, and cinnamon, when sautéed in oil, emit deep, enticing aromas that build anticipation long before you take the first bite.

Mindful Smelling Exercise: A Guided Practice for Full Sensory Presence

Before we even take that first bite, let's pause and fully embrace the act of smelling. Ready? Find yourself a quiet moment, a plate of food, and take a deep breath. Now, close your eyes. Bring the food close to your nose and inhale deeply. Take a slow, luxurious breath—feel the scent filling your senses. Can you identify the notes? Is it fresh, earthy, sweet, or spicy?

Take a moment to notice how the scent affects your body. Does it make your mouth water? Does it bring back a memory or evoke an emotion? Allow yourself to truly savor this seductive moment before the flavor hits your tongue. The more you engage your senses, the more you will awaken your body to the full experience of eating.

As you continue this practice, you'll find that the smells deepen your enjoyment, transforming each meal into something more than just nourishment. It becomes a ritual, a sensory embrace that enhances everything—the taste, the texture, the pleasure of the moment.

The next time you sit down for a meal, remember: smell is the invitation to taste. Don't rush it. Take a moment, breathe deeply, and let the aromas work their magic. The experience will be nothing short of intoxicating.

Taste – The Fulfilling Sense of Flavor

When we talk about food, we're really talking about flavor. And the key to flavor? Taste. It's the magic ingredient that turns a bite of food into an experience. We can all remember that first bite of something sweet, salty, or bitter, and how it made us pause, linger, and even smile. Taste is more than just a sensation—it's an invitation to indulge, to savor, to explore. But how do we truly unlock the full power of taste? Well, let's start with the basics: the five essential tastes that shape the way we experience food.

The 4 Basic Tastes: Sweet, Salty, Sour, Bitter

Have you noticed our tongues are pretty incredible little organs? They have five primary taste receptors, each one serving up a unique sensation. Let's break them down:

1. Sweet: Ah, our favorite, sweetness, the most universally loved of all tastes. It's what we crave when we reach for that chocolate bar or take that first bite of a ripe, juicy peach. Sweetness signals energy, which is why our bodies love it so much. But sweetness isn't just about sugar. It can come from natural sources like fruits, honey, or even vegetables like carrots or sweet potatoes.

2. Salty: Saltiness enhances flavors, drawing out depth and richness. It's a little like that flirtatious wink across the room, it adds a touch of mischief. Salt helps balance sweetness and masks bitterness, which is why a pinch of salt in desserts can make the flavors pop. Too little salt, and your food feels flat; too much, and it overwhelms everything. Salt, when used right, is the life of the party.

3. Sour: Then there is sourness. It's sharp, it's edgy, and it keeps us on our toes. A squeeze of lemon over grilled fish or a bite of tangy yogurt can wake up your taste buds like nothing else. Sourness comes from acidic foods, like citrus, vinegar, and even fermented foods like kimchi or pickles. It cuts through richness, balances sweetness, and adds complexity to a dish.

4. Bitter: Think of a strong coffee, dark chocolate, or cilantro; bitter flavors add a layer of sophistication and depth. They help to ground the dish and bring a balance to the sweetness and saltiness. As you know bitter flavors aren't for everyone, but when done right, they can elevate the experience from simple to sophisticated.

These four tastes do not exist in isolation. They mingle, dance, and play off one another to create complex flavor profiles in every dish. A perfect balance of sweet, salty, sour, and bitter, is the key to a dish that satisfies not just your appetite but your soul.

Cultural and Personal Taste Preferences: How the Environment and Experience Shape How We Enjoy food

Well, here's the thing: our relationship with taste is deeply personal and influenced by culture, environment, and experience. Growing up in a family where spicy food was the norm might make you crave heat with every meal, while someone raised on milder fare may find the intensity overwhelming. Our surroundings, childhood memories, and even our cultural backgrounds shape the flavors we love and the ones we're not so crazy about.

This diversity in preferences is what makes food so incredibly exciting. The beauty of cooking is that it allows you to experiment with these taste profiles and create something that speaks to your unique taste palate.

Tasting Techniques: How to Savor and Identify Individual Flavors in Food

Lastly, let's talk about savoring food like a true connoisseur. Tasting food isn't just about putting it in your mouth and swallowing, it's about taking your time. When you take a bite of food, take a moment to pause, close your eyes, and really experience the layers of flavor unfolding. First, pay attention to the "first impression", the initial burst of flavor. Is it sweet? salty? sour? Then, notice how the flavor evolves. Does it become richer, spicier, or more savory as it lingers? And finally, reflect on the aftertaste or how the flavor sticks around, how it changes once the food leaves your mouth.

When you continue to practice this you'll develop a sophisticated palate, able to discern the individual flavors and how they work together. Soon, you'll find yourself savoring not just the food but the full sensory experience; the sounds, the textures, and the smells all working in harmony to create something truly unforgettable.

Touch – Texture and Mouth Feel

Imagine if you will, a perfectly roasted chicken thigh, its skin crackling with that glorious, golden crisp, and underneath, the tender, juicy meat that practically melts in your mouth. Or a ripe, succulent kiwi, its smooth, silky flesh giving way to a burst of sweet juice. These are moments of pure sensual pleasure and not just about taste, no, they're about "texture". The way food feels in your mouth can transform an ordinary meal into a full-bodied experience, one that taps into our primal senses and satisfies in ways we often overlook. This chapter is all about "mouthfeel", that luxurious, irresistible sensation that food gives us when we bite, chew, or swallow.

Why Texture Matters: The Science of Mouthfeel and How It Affects Flavor Perception

We often talk about taste, but let's not forget about mouthfeel, the term that describes how food physically feels in our mouths. It's that first bite of a soft, pillowy freshly baked bread roll or the satisfying snap of a fresh vegetable. I found out that texture isn't just a side note in the symphony of our senses; it's a key player. In fact, studies have shown that the texture of food can significantly enhance our perception of its flavor.

Think about it: the creamy texture of a ripe avocado or the crunch of a crisp leaf of lettuce enhances the flavor experience, which is amazing right!? The smoother the texture, the richer the flavor often seems. On the other hand, something with fiber or a slight grit can take the edge off a flavor's intensity, offering a subtle contrast that's both interesting and satisfying.

This is why we as humans associate the best foods with mouthfeel as much as taste, there's something seductive about the right texture. Crunchy, creamy, chewy, or tender, the assorted textures in food often creates a certain pleasure that can elevate our eating experience from something mundane to something deeply satisfying. When we bite into a perfectly cooked piece of steak, you're not just tasting it; you're marinating in the tender juiciness and the way it falls apart just enough to be indulgent, yet firm enough to feel more than adequate.

Eating with the Hands: Cultural Perspectives and the Sensory Benefits of Tactile Eating

If anything, food is an experience that begins well before the first bite. It starts with the touch. In many cultures, eating with your hands isn't just accepted, it's encouraged. From India to parts of the Middle East and Africa, using your hands to eat connects you directly to the food, heightening the sensory experience and your overall submersion in the culture. When you pick up a piece of naan or a juicy lamb kebab with your hands, you don't just taste the food; you feel it. It is important that you can sense its warmth, its texture, and even the moisture that clings to it. This tactile engagement enhances the flavor and makes the meal more intimate, personal, and foundational.

As you will learn, eating with your hands taps into something ancient within us, something that makes us slow down and be present with our food. You can feel the softness of warm bread, the stickiness of rice, the flame kissed texture of grilled meats. Each and every touch becomes a more sensual experience, inviting you to linger longer on every bite. It's no surprise that in some cultures, food eaten with the hands is considered the most sensual and satisfying way to eat because it encourages you to embrace the textures in ways that utensils just can't.

Mindful Texture Exploration: Exercises for Experiencing Texture in Both Solid Foods and Liquids

Now, let's take a moment to get truly intimate with our food. Let's explore the textures in a way that makes us "feel" each bite, rather than just chew and swallow. The next time you sit down for a meal, do a little experiment with yourself. Just close your eyes for a moment before you dig in. Take a piece of food, like a ripe apple, a warm piece of bread, or a smooth spoonful of yogurt, and let your fingers explore it. Take a moment to feel its surface. Is it smooth or full of bumps? Soft or firm? Is it sticky or dry? This simple exercise can deepen your connection to the food and make the eating experience even more pleasurable.

Now, go ahead and take a bite and pay attention to how it feels in your mouth. Take note of the sensation as you chew, the way it breaks apart, the temperature, the amount of moisture in its content. When we eat something like a piece of chocolate, notice the smoothness as it melts, the way the texture transforms. If you're sipping a hot beverage, feel how the liquid coats your mouth and throat. Pay attention to how different foods "feel"; trust me, it's a game-changer.

Hopefully you have found out that texture isn't just a side note in eating, it's an essential part of the experience that makes food so sensual, exciting, and satisfying. Whether it's the crunch of a crisp vegetable, the creamy silkiness of a perfectly ripe avocado, or the tender melt-in-your-mouth quality of a slow-cooked stew, the textures in food do more than just add to its taste; they elevate it. So, the next time you sit down to eat a meal, make it a point to embrace the textures. Try to feel the food before you taste it. Go ahead and let your hands connect with it, and let your mouth explore every nuance of that glorious mouthfeel. Because when you eat with your senses fully engaged, you're not just feeding your body, you're indulging your soul.

Sound – The Underestimated Sense

Now let's talk about the sounds of your environment. Not just the kind you hear from the latest pop hits or the hum of traffic outside your window, but the sounds of food, the sizzle, the crunch, the slurp. Yes, you heard me right. Sound is an often overlooked sense when it comes to eating, but trust me, it's an essential player in the overall experience. Too often we focus so much on what food looks like or how it tastes, but what if I told you that the right sound can elevate your meal in ways you've never dreamed?

The Role of Sound in Eating: How Crunch, Sizzle, and Other Sounds Influence Enjoyment

Have you ever taken a moment to listen to that irresistible sizzle of a steak hitting a hot pan, the way the sound dances around your kitchen? It's not just the heat doing its thing; it's your brain already beginning to salivate, prepped for the flavor that's about to explode when that first bite is taken. The crunch of a perfectly fried chip, the snap of a fresh cucumber, it's all part of the dance, baby. These sounds are crucial because they trigger immediate sensory responses. The sound of food isn't just noise; it's a prelude to the pleasure that's about to unfold with each bite.

Stop and think about it: have you ever eaten something that in your mind was supposed to be crispy but was just... soggy? That wet, mushy sound when you bite into something that should have had more texture? It's off-putting, right? The wrong sound can totally sabotage your experience. It's why that first crisp bite of a delicious red apple is so satisfying. Sound connects us to our expectations, and when those expectations are met, and when the sound matches the taste, we are in sensory heaven.

Influences of Background Sound and Music: How Ambient Sounds Affect Taste Perception and Mood

Now, let's go ahead and throw another layer into the mix: background sound. Oh yes, music and ambient noises can radically change how you experience food. For instance, have you ever noticed that your favorite playlist seems to enhance the flavor of a glass of wine or make your meal feel even more decadent? There's real science behind that. Some studies show that music can influence the way we perceive flavor. Softer, slower music tends to make food taste smoother, while upbeat, fast-paced music can give food a little more zip. The dulcet tones and rhythm of the tune plays on our sensory memory, adjusting how our brain processes flavors.

The atmosphere matters too. A bustling, lively restaurant might make a crispy pizza taste even more vibrant because of the ambient noise, the chatter, the clinking glasses, the low hum of voices. It's like being wrapped in the energy of the space, and that vibrancy influences the food. On the other hand, a quiet, intimate dinner at home, with the right gentle background music, can transform your meal into something luxurious, more mindful. With this case in particular, silence brings out the subtleties of your food's flavor. It allows you to focus on the layers of taste, the sweetness of the tomatoes, the saltiness of the cheese, and the richness of the sauce. The sound (or lack of it) shapes the way you experience the overall meal.

As I found out, sound is a key player in the dance of eating, a seductive, often-ignored aspect of flavor that we should all embrace. Whether it's the crunch of a perfect fry, the sizzle of a hot pan, or the music playing softly in the background, the right sound enhances your meal. So the next time you sit down to eat, listen carefully. Your senses are talking, and the food's luscious melody is just waiting to be heard.

The Multi-Sensory Experience: Bringing It All Together

Now we must talk again about food—not just as fuel, but as an experience. Try to Imagine sinking into a chair at a beautiful set table, the world outside muffled, the air rich with aromas. As the waiter places the plate In front of you, think of it as a feast for the senses, where every bite, every sound, every texture comes together in a delicate dance. Food, when experienced this way, becomes something so much more than just a taste. It's a sensual journey. It's the synergy of sight, smell, taste, touch, and sound, each sense working in harmony to elevate the meal to a whole new level. So, let's just dive into this multi sensory adventure, where every element interacts, enhances, and deepens the overall experience.

The Cohesive Synergy of the Senses: How sight, smell, taste, touch, and sound interact to create a unique eating experience.

As we now know each of our five senses plays a distinct role in shaping our relationship with food, but what happens when it all comes together? I'll tell you what happens, it becomes MAGIC! The sheer beauty of a plate of food is the first thing that catches your eye, the vibrant colors, the artful arrangement. The next thing you know your mind starts to form expectations even before the first bite. Think of it, as you bring that fork to your lips, you inhale the fragrance. The scent alone could make you salivate, in a longing anticipation of the glorious flavor to come.

But wait, there's a twist: sight and smell can trick the brain into thinking something tastes better than it actually does. That's why a decadent chocolate mousse feels richer, or a fresh berry picked straight from the vine bursts with sweetness. Our brains are wired to connect to those senses. So when everything aligns, like a luscious red strawberry that appears to be perfectly ripe, smells fresh and earthy, and tastes sweet on your tongue, truly makes the experience abundantly more satisfying.

Then the texture is where things get even more exciting. Imagine biting into a perfectly seared piece of fish. The amazing crunch of the crispy skin contrasts with the tender, buttery flesh inside, creating a cohesive collaboration between the smooth and the crispy, the soft and the firm. It's a tactile dance, where your mouth becomes the stage and the food is the performer.

And then there's the sound. The subtle sizzle of a steak hitting a hot pan. The crunch of fresh vegetables under your bite. The soft, melodic sound of wine being poured into a glass. These auditory cues don't just add ambiance; they set the tone and heighten our sensory anticipation, making the meal feel even more immersive and satisfying.

The Concept of "Flavor Pairing": Why Some Foods Naturally Taste Better Together Through Sensory Harmony

Ok, now let's talk about why certain combinations of food make your taste buds sing. It's not just magic—well, maybe a little—but it's mostly science. You will notice that flavor pairing is all about balance and sensory harmony. Think about the contrast between the sweetness of ripe fruit and the tang of fresh cheese. A perfectly ripe pear with a sharp blue cheese is a match made in heaven, and here's why: the sweetness of the pear mellows the boldness of the cheese, while the saltiness of the cheese brings out the fruit's natural juiciness. It's this kind of interaction between flavors, textures, and aromas that creates a greater experience as it incorporates the whole sum of its parts.

For instance, take a classic Italian pairing, prosciutto and melon. The salty, savory flavor of the prosciutto is balanced perfectly by the sweet juiciness of the melon. Together, they also create a contrast of textures as well: the smooth, slippery melon against the chewiness of the prosciutto. The flavors aren't just complementary, they enhance each other, it is truly a symbiotic relationship..

As you understand the concept of flavor pairing, you can get creative in the kitchen, creating your own sensory symphonies. Balancing salty with sweet, hot with cold, creamy with crunchy. The beauty of flavor pairing is that it's both an art and a science, as you become more aware of it you'll never look at food the same way again.

The synergy of sight, smell, taste, touch, and sound creates a feast that's far beyond mere nourishment. It's a way of living, eating, and feeling. So, next time you sit down to eat, remember: it's not just about the flavor. It's about the entire experience, the multi sensory magic happens when we slow down and savor it all.

Mindfulness and Eating for Well-being

You know, food is incredibly seductive when you approach it with your full attention. It's not just the flavors, the textures, or the aromas it's the act of truly connecting with the taste and savoring every moment. As we eat mindfully, we slow down and connect not only with the food in front of us but also with our bodies and desires. Mindful eating isn't just about following a diet or counting calories, it's about truly experiencing food in all its glory. So how about we dive into how sensory awareness can transform our eating habits, boost our overall well-being, and leave us feeling more satisfied than we ever imagined.

Mindful Eating Practices: How sensory awareness can promote healthier, more satisfying eating habits.

Now here is one of the greatest benefits of slowing down while eating. The way it makes us feel. Not just because it's good for you, but because it feels downright indulgent, like a slow, deliberate, indulgent affair where every bite is savored, when every moment is stretched just a little bit longer. That's what mindful eating is all about. Instead of rushing through your meal or letting your mind wander to the next thing on your to-do list, mindful eating invites you to really "be" with your food.

It begins by awakening all of the senses, your eyes, your nose, your fingers, your tongue. Notice the color of your plate, the shape of your vegetables, the glisten of a perfectly seared steak. Breathe in the aroma, the earthy richness of garlic, the sweetness of fresh fruit, or the smokiness of grilled meat. Go ahead and feel the texture in your mouth, the crunch of a crispy crust, the smoothness of a ripe avocado. All of this sensory exploration isn't just for pleasure; it's for your health too. Studies show that eating mindfully can lead to healthier eating habits by allowing you to tune into your body's hunger and fullness cues. The result? You will be less likely to overeat by not allowing your emotions to influence how much you eat.

By paying close attention to the sensations of eating, you will naturally become more attuned to what your body really craves, and what it doesn't really need. This type of mindfulness transforms eating from a mechanical task to an experience that nourishes both your body and your soul. The simple act of slowing down allows you to enjoy your food on a deeper level, making every meal a celebration.

Eating with Gratitude: How Appreciating Food Positively Affects Enjoyment and Digestion

But there's a lot more to mindful eating than just awareness, it's about appreciation. When you sit down to a meal and truly appreciate the food in front of you, something magical happens. It becomes more than just fuel. It becomes a gift, a treasure you've been given to nourish and delight in. This is where gratitude enters the picture.

Gratitude has the power to transform your eating experience. It shifts your mindset from not just consuming nourishment, but truly appreciating it. Before you take your first bite, pause for a moment. Think about all the hands that have touched this food before it reached you. The farmers who grew the vegetables, the artisans who crafted the bread, the fresh markets where the ingredients were sourced. Then, when you take that first bite, let yourself feel thankful. Let your senses revel in the flavors, the textures, the memories the food might evoke. When you take a moment and eat with gratitude, you create a deeper connection with the meal, and that connection heightens the senses and elevates the enjoyment.

Plus there are more benefits. Gratitude has been shown to improve digestion, too. When you're stressed or distracted, your body doesn't digest food properly, it's in "fight or flight" mode. But when you eat with a sense of calm and appreciation, your body shifts into a "rest and digest" state. This means your food is processed more efficiently, nutrients are absorbed better, and your body relaxes and feels nourished on a deeper level.

Reducing Stress Through Sensory Eating: Techniques for Using the Senses to Slow Down and Relax During Meals

Now, let's talk about the way eating can assist you and help you to unwind. In our fast-paced world, stress is almost inevitable, but there's a deliciously simple way to counteract it: eating mindfully. When you're under pressure, your body is flooded with stress hormones that affect everything from your mood to your digestion. But by using the senses to slow down during meals, you can signal your body to relax and take in the moment before you.

Let's start by creating a peaceful atmosphere. Set the table with intention, maybe you would light a candle or play soft music in the background. When you sit down to eat, take in a deep breath and slowly release it. Focus on the colors and shapes of the food in front of you. Then, take another breath, letting the smells of your meal fill your senses. This simple practice will begin to lower your stress levels almost immediately. The more you make a habit of eating in a calm, sensory-focused way, the more you'll feel the benefits on your body and your mind.

An additional technique is to engage your sense of touch. Let yourself feel the warmth of your cup of tea or the smoothness of a ripe peach in your hand. The simple act of touching your food can ground you in the moment, slowing down your racing thoughts. The slower you eat, the less stress you carry into your body. It's ok to give yourself permission to savor, to relax, to fully enjoy.

So we have found the secret: we now know that eating doesn't have to be a rushed or thoughtless act. When we approach food with intention, awareness, and gratitude, we can transform eating into an experience that nourishes both the body and the soul. By engaging all your senses and allowing ourselves to be fully present with our food, and in turn, our lives. So go ahead, take a breath, slow down, and indulge in the sensual joy of eating. It's a practice that will leave you feeling more connected, more relaxed, and more satisfied with every bite.

Sensory Eating Around The World

Try to Imagine savoring a warm, golden samosa straight from the bustling streets of India, the pastry is crisp against your fingertips and the aroma of spices is filling the air around you. Now, think of a delicate Japanese tea ceremony, the earthy fragrance of matcha, the smooth texture of the ceramic cup, the simple ritualistic movements that draw you into an experience that's more about savoring life than it is about sipping tea. All around the world, different cultures have mastered the art of sensory eating, turning food into a whole-body experience. Now let's explore how different traditions use sensory eating to make meals so much more than just food on a plate.

Global Perspectives on Eating with the Senses

In many cultures around the world, sensory eating takes on very distinct forms, but the goal is the same: to connect deeply with the experience of culinary indulgence. In Japan, for instance, food presentation is an art in itself. The meals are crafted with aesthetics in mind; they're designed to engage the eyes before any of the other senses. Japanese dishes are colorful and beautifully arranged, balancing colors, shapes, and garnishes that mirror the natural world. This attention to visual detail primes the mind to enjoy the flavors that are to follow, creating a harmony of sight and taste that's intentional and captivating.

In contrast, Indian cuisine invites you to dive in only using your hands. For many people eating with your hands may feel unusual, but for India, it is believed to create a connection between the person dining and the food, almost like a final handshake with the chef that created it. Take note as your fingers press into fluffy naan or scooped up dal, you feel the texture, the warmth, the softness or crispiness, all of these elements enhance the experience and bring a more visceral profile to the abundant flavors.

Meanwhile, in Italy, the sensory experience of food is often shared. Italians prioritize meals as a time to connect and engage with others, so even a simple antipasto becomes a symphony of sights, smells, and tastes shared across the table.

An antipasto platter is a feast for the senses: vibrant tomatoes, salty olives, fragrant cheeses, and cured meats, all arranged to be savored, shared, and celebrated. Even the scents seem to mingle and flavors gently contrast, encouraging diners to sample each morsel in a rhythm that's just as social as it is sensory.

Each of the previous cultures have dishes and rituals that highlight sensory engagement, transforming meals into joyous celebrations of the many facets of life's flavors and textures. Japanese tea ceremonies, for instance, go far beyond drinking tea. From the slow pouring to the warm, grassy aroma of matcha, to the soft, quiet sound of the whisk in the bowl, the ceremony offers an opportunity to be fully present. It's as much about savoring the tea's texture and smell as it is about embracing the peacefulness and artistic nature of the moment.

Learning from Tradition: How cultural practices can inspire a more sensory approach to everyday eating.

These eating traditions are more than just cultural practices, they're guides for embracing life. Taking a cue from Japan, we can start our meals by appreciating the visual elements of the food. We can notice the colors, shapes, and even the contrast between the elements. From India, we can learn to engage the tactile sense, by picking up a piece of bread and feeling its texture before taking a bite. And from Italy, we're reminded that meals are best enjoyed in good company, with plenty of laughter and hearty conversation that make every flavor profile so much richer.

Cultivating a Life of Sensory Eating

Go ahead and start small. Every time you sit down, take a moment to appreciate the colors and shapes on your plate. Just close your eyes and take in the scent of your food. Notice the food's warmth against your lips, the slight crunch, the burst of flavor on your tongue. Now try savoring each bite without a feeling of urgency which only invites pleasure, fullness, and connection and offers the ability to be present in a given moment.

Go ahead, give it a try: tonight, let yourself be fully present with your meal. Put away any and all distractions. With each bite, notice what textures and flavors emerge. Take a deep breath between bites, allowing the pleasure to linger. This is your life, your taste, your unique journey with food. If we all would approach eating this way, we would find that the most ordinary moments are transformed into extraordinary ones. Let this be your personal practice, a playful, delicious commitment to yourself, where each meal becomes a celebration of life, and evolves into a love letter to your senses.

I think we have learned to Imagine every meal as a seduction of the senses. Eating with awareness is not just about taking a bite, it's about letting yourself feel, smell, hear, and see every element of your food through a multidimensional lens like a lover's caress. It's a lifelong romance with the flavors, textures, and aromas that grace your plate. When we take the opportunity to slow down, even the simplest meals become sumptuous experiences, a dance of sensation that nourishes us from the inside out and from the outside in. Bon Appetit!

Dear Reader,

Thank you so much for choosing The Sensual Art of Eating! I truly hope this book brings you as much joy and insight as it did for me while writing it. Your support means the world, and I'd love to hear your thoughts. If you enjoyed the journey, please consider leaving a review—it helps others discover the experience too.

With gratitude,

B.D. Mack

REFERENCES

Brillat-Savarin, J. A. (2023). *The physiology of taste; or, transcendental gastronomy: in large print.* BoD – Books on Demand.

Briscione, J., & Parkhurst, B. (2018). *The flavor matrix: The Art and Science of Pairing Common Ingredients to Create Extraordinary Dishes.* Houghton Mifflin Harcourt.

Cook, G. (2015). Dan Jurafsky: The Language of Food: A linguist reads the menu. *Applied Linguistics, 37*(1), 139–142. https://doi.org/10.1093/applin/amv021

DeSilva, C. (1996). *In Memory's kitchen: A Legacy from the Women of Terezin.* Jason Aronson.

Dewalt, K. M. (2013). The Omnivorous Mind: Our Evolving Relationship With Food Edited by John S. Allen. Cambridge, MA: Harvard University Press. 2012. 319 pp. ISBN 978-0-674-05572-8. $29.95 (Paper). *American Journal of Physical Anthropology, 151*(1), 164–165. https://doi.org/10.1002/ajpa.22251

Donovan, M. M. (2018). Mindful Eating: A guide to rediscovering a healthy and joyful relationship with food. *Journal of Nutrition Education and Behavior, 50*(7), 752. https://doi.org/10.1016/j.jneb.2018.02.010

Ellena, J. (2011). *Perfume: The Alchemy of Scent.* Skyhorse.

Fisher, M. F. K. (2004). *The art of eating.* Houghton Mifflin Harcourt.

Gil-Pérez, I., Rebollar, R., Lidón, I., Martín, J., Van Trijp, H. C., & Piqueras-Fiszman, B. (2018). Hot or not? Conveying sensory information on food packaging through the spiciness-shape correspondence. *Food Quality and Preference, 71,* 197–208. https://doi.org/10.1016/j.foodqual.2018.07.009

Hanh, T. N., & Cheung, L. (2011). *Mindful eating, mindful life: Savour every moment and every bite.* Hay House, Inc.

Holmes, B. (2017). *Flavor: the science of our most neglected sense.* W. W. Norton & Company.

Lupton, E., & Lipps, A. (2018). *The Senses: Design Beyond Vision.* Chronicle Books.

Nosrat, S. (2017). *Salt, fat, acid, heat: Mastering the Elements of Good Cooking.* Simon and Schuster.

Piqueras-Fiszman, B., & Spence, C. (2016). *Multisensory flavor perception: From Fundamental Neuroscience Through to the Marketplace.* Woodhead Publishing.

Prescott, J. (2013). *Taste matters: Why We Like the Foods We Do.* Reaktion Books.

Puddicombe, A. (2012). *The headspace guide to. . . Mindful Eating.* Hachette UK.

Rachão, S., Breda, Z., Fernandes, C., & Joukes, V. (2019). Food tourism and regional development: A systematic literature review. *European Journal of Tourism Research, 21*, 33–49. https://doi.org/10.54055/ejtr.v21i.357

Rosenthal, A. J., & Thompson, P. (2021). What is cohesiveness?—A linguistic exploration of the food texture testing literature. *Journal of Texture Studies, 52*(3), 294–302. https://doi.org/10.1111/jtxs.12586

Shepherd, G. (2013). *Neurogastronomy: How the Brain Creates Flavor and Why It Matters.* Columbia University Press.

This, H. (2006). *Molecular Gastronomy: Exploring the Science of Flavor.* Columbia University Press.

Ubbink, J. (2017a). There's more to a meal Gastrophysics: The New Science of Eating Charles Spence Viking, 2017. 336 pp. *Science, 356*(6343), 1129. https://doi.org/10.1126/science.aan4039

Ubbink, J. (2017b). There's more to a meal Gastrophysics: The New Science of Eating Charles Spence Viking, 2017. 336 pp. *Science, 356*(6343), 1129. https://doi.org/10.1126/science.aan4039

Waters, A. (2021). *We Are What We Eat: A Slow Food Manifesto.*

Wilson, B. (2018, February 22). Gastrophysics: The New Science of Eating by Charles Spence – review. *The Guardian.* https://www.theguardian.com/books/2017/mar/23/gastrophysics-new-science-eating-charles-spence-review